SAUDI ARABIA
in Pictures

VGS

Catherine Broberg

Lerner Publications Company

Contents

Website address: www.lernerbooks.com

Lerner Publications Company
A division of Lerner Publishing Group
241 First Avenue North
Minneapolis, MN 55401 U.S.A.

web enhanced @ www.vgsbooks.com

Library of Congress Cataloging-in-Publication Data

Broberg, Catherine.
    Saudi Arabia in pictures / by Catherine Broberg.—Rev. & expanded.
        p.   cm. — [Visual geography series]
    Includes bibliographical references and index.
    ISBN: 0-8225-1958-5 (lib. bdg. : alk. paper)
    1. Saudi Arabia—Juvenile literature. 2. Saudi Arabia—Pictorial works. I. Title. II. Visual geography series
[Minneapolis, Minn.]
DS204.25 B76 2003
953.8—dc21   2001002967

Manufactured in the United States of America
1 2 3 4 5 6 - JR - 08 07 06 05 04 03

INTRODUCTION

As the twenty-first century begins, the Kingdom of Saudi Arabia—which occupies 80 percent of the Arabian Peninsula—seeks to find balance between its dedication to the religious faith of Islam and its role in the modern world. Saudi Arabia was founded as an Islamic nation with a government based on the laws of Islam. The practice of Islam's traditions has not declined with time; rather, daily life in this desert country still revolves around prayer. On the other hand, life in Saudi Arabia has changed substantially since oil was discovered there in the late 1930s. Saudi Arabia's subsequent oil wealth propelled it into the industrial world, a world that includes modern technology, development, and other influences from North America and Europe.

A typical street scene in Saudi Arabia illustrates the country's struggles between old and new. Modern concrete and steel buildings stand near adobe houses, and cars and donkeys jostle for position on newly built roads. Muezzins (criers), who call Muslims (followers of Islam) to prayer, blend with radios that play hit songs. Amid these con-

trasts, Saudi Arabia works to develop a modern yet traditionally Islamic nation.

With the revenue that oil produces, Saudi Arabia has become a powerful and active member in the community of Middle Eastern nations. One of the charter members of the Arab League—an organization founded in 1945 to promote closer ties among Arab countries— Saudi Arabia has often been a leader in the league's council meetings.

In 1960, to gain better control of its rapidly growing petroleum industry, Saudi Arabia joined with the South American country of Venezuela to invite other oil-producing nations to form the Organization of Petroleum Exporting Countries (OPEC). This group works to establish oil prices and oil production quotas beneficial to its members, and Saudi Arabia plays a pivotal role in OPEC's negotiations.

In the 1980s, the war between Iran and Iraq—large nations bordering the Persian Gulf—threatened the stability of the Arab region. The

Saudi Arabia is a **country full of contrasts.** In this picture, a driver of a modern car passes a museum whose design is based on traditional Islamic architecture.

conflict also hindered the transportation of oil to world markets. In 1990 and early 1991, Saudi Arabia again became involved in an armed conflict, the Persian Gulf War, after Iraq invaded Kuwait, a small neighboring country. A coalition of U.S., European, and Middle Eastern forces used bases in northern Saudi Arabia during the war, which ended with the liberation of Kuwait.

Terrorist attacks in New York City and Washington, D.C., on September 11, 2001, again brought world attention to Saudi Arabia and its neighbors. The horrifying attacks, which killed thousands of people, were widely believed to have been supported by Osama bin Laden, a former Saudi citizen based, at the time, in Afghanistan. In facing this international crisis, Saudi Arabia was challenged to maintain a careful balance between supporting the antiterrorist efforts of the United States—a longtime ally—and protecting the interests and sensitivities of its Muslim population. This balance of interests is likely to become increasingly significant as Saudi Arabia grapples with the forces of technology and globalization in the twenty-first century.

THE LAND

Saudi Arabia contains approximately 865,000 square miles (2,240,000 square kilometers) of territory—an area about the size of the United States from the East Coast to the Mississippi River. Although it is a very large country, much of Saudi Arabia is inhospitable desert with little or no rainfall. The Red Sea forms Saudi Arabia's western frontier, and Jordan, Iraq, and Kuwait lie to the north. To the east are the Persian (Arabian) Gulf, Qatar, and the United Arab Emirates. Yemen and Oman are Saudi Arabia's southern neighbors. Many of the area's boundaries, particularly in the south, run through remote, barren areas. The borders between Saudi Arabia and its southern neighbors have historically been undefined. Beginning in the mid-1990s, however, Saudi Arabia has established border agreements with these countries. In 1995 Saudi Arabia and Oman signed agreements to define their joint border. The long-standing border dispute with Qatar was resolved in 1999. And in June 2000, Saudi Arabia and Yemen signed a treaty defining the land and sea boundaries between the two countries.

▶ Topography

The Arabian Peninsula, which is composed mostly of Saudi Arabia, slopes downward from the west to the east. The region has mountains on its western edge, large areas of desert, and no permanent above-ground supplies of water. Saudi Arabia can be divided into five main geographical areas: Hejaz and Asir, Nejd, Rub al-Khali, al-Nafud, and al-Hasa (also called the Eastern Province).

The mountainous western coast of Saudi Arabia is made up of the Hejaz region in the north and the Asir region in the south. In Hejaz the mountains average about 7,000 feet (2135 meters) above sea level and often drop abruptly into the sea, leaving very little area of coastal plain and very few navigable harbors. Most settlements lie on the more gently sloping eastern side of the mountains, where oases (watered areas) are located.

A gap in the mountains near the city of Mecca interrupts the coastal range and marks the end of Hejaz and the beginning of the

Farmers **terrace the land** for planting crops in the southwestern Asir region of Saudi Arabia.

Asir region. The coastal plain is broader in this southern region, sometimes reaching almost 40 miles (64 km) in width, and the mountains are generally higher than those in Hejaz. Asir is the most fertile region of Saudi Arabia. Farmers cultivate its coastal strip and carve terraces (horizontal ridges) into its mountains to create level farmland.

The mountains of Hejaz and Asir taper off to the east into large, irregular plateaus. This rocky area—called Nejd—occupies central Saudi Arabia and contains a few small deserts and some isolated mountains. Wadis—dry riverbeds that carry water from brief seasonal rains— run eastward toward the Persian Gulf. In the middle of Nejd lies the Tuwayq Mountains, a long series of ridges that rise from 300 to 900 feet (90 to 275 m) above the plateau.

North of Nejd is the al-Nafud desert, with sand dunes that extend for miles. The sand contains a high level of iron oxide, which often gives it a red tint. Very few oases exist in this desert, and very little rain falls. When winter rains come, scrub grasses grow for a brief period. Nomadic herders bring their flocks to feed on the short-lived plants in early spring.

To the south of Nejd lies the huge Rub al-Khali, or Empty Quarter. The largest sand desert in the world, this region is nearly uninhabited, and years may pass before rain falls. Approximately 250,000 square miles (648,000 sq. km) in area, Rub al-Khali is almost as big as the state of Texas.

In the east, along the Persian Gulf, lies the coastal plain of al-Hasa. Made up of sand and gravel plains, al-Hasa—the source of Saudi Arabia's vast oil wealth—holds the largest known deposits of petroleum in the world.

The Oases

Except for wadis, the bed of a stream that contain water only during the rainy season, Saudi Arabia does not have any rivers or lakes. Other waterways include the small canals dug next to wells that transport water to the fields. The country gets its water primarily from underground sources and through the technology of desalination (a process of removing the salt from seawater). Two pipelines, with a total combined length of 290 miles (467 km), carry desalinated water between the cities of Jubail and Riyadh, Saudi Arabia's capital city. The pipelines have the capacity to carry 210 million gallons (795 million liters) of water each day.

An oasis is an island of greenery in an otherwise barren desert. Its fertility is caused by underground springs or wells, and the amount of water that is available determines the size of the oasis. Some oases consist of a few palm trees around a muddy water hole and support only temporary inhabitants. Other oases cover a number of square miles and enable a permanent population of several thousand people

An old fort stands amid lush greenery in an oasis.

to live nearby. Oasis dwellers raise camels, sheep, and goats and grow a variety of vegetables and fruits.

In places where the water supply is sufficient to last an entire year, large-scale agriculture takes place. Rainwater, which is quickly absorbed by the sand and gravel, feeds some wells. Other wells are maintained by underground supplies that were formed millions of years ago. By digging more wells and by setting up irrigation systems, the Saudi government has created many artificial oases. These areas make it possible for people to settle permanently in the desert and to grow their own food.

Climate

Saudi Arabia has a very dry, hot climate with frequent dust storms and sandstorms. Summer temperatures can rise to 130°F (54°C) during the day, dropping to about 30° to 40°F (−1° to 4°C) at night. Temperatures along the coasts of the Red Sea and the Persian Gulf are not as uncomfortable, but the humidity is much higher, particularly near the Persian Gulf, which is known for its frequent, heavy fogs.

In a country with very dry air and high temperatures, air-conditioning has become commonplace and, for many, a necessity. During the hot summer months, air conditioning accounts for as much as 70 percent of the energy consumed in Saudi Arabia.

In the central and northern parts of the country, temperatures seldom drop below freezing in the winter. Riyadh is cool in the winter, with daytime temperatures dropping as low as 50°F (10°C). In July the temperature averages 93°F (32°C).

The average annual rainfall for the country is 4 inches (10 centimeters). Often an entire year's rain comes in one or two downpours between October and March. The Asir region receives the most rain—12 to 20 inches (30 to 50 cm)—while some areas, such as the Rub al-Khali, receive no rain for many years in a row.

Flora

Vegetation in Saudi Arabia is generally sparse because of lack of rain and poor soil. Trees are a rare sight and are completely absent in most areas. The country's only forests are made up of wild olive and juniper trees, which grow in the mountains of the Asir region. Small shrubs and herbs—especially plants of the mustard and chamomile families—are common. Most plants have adapted to the conditions of desert existence, some by reducing their leaf surface area. For example, plants with spiny or needlelike leaves lose less water from evaporation.

Other plants have the ability to store water, and some are even able to take nourishment from salt water.

Among small trees and shrubs that have adapted to the desert climate are the aloe plant and the tamarisk tree, both of which are found in much of the country. At high altitudes, fig trees and carob trees (an evergreen with red flowers) flourish, as well as cactuslike euphorbias.

Wildflowers are abundant at high elevations, particularly during the rainy season. Reeds provide material for building small dwellings and for thatching roofs. In the deserts, widely scattered shrubs grow, especially the *hadh*, a kind of saltbush.

Fauna

Small, swift gazelles and large-horned oryx (a type of antelope) once roamed freely in Saudi Arabia but are rarely seen in modern times. Efforts are being made to reintroduce these animals into the region. Meat eaters—such as wolves, hyenas, and jackals—can be found, and smaller mammals include foxes, ratels (badgerlike animals), rabbits, hedgehogs, and jerboas (rodents with long hind legs). Ibex (wild goats) live in the mountains of the Hejaz region, and baboons populate the highlands of Asir.

The most important animal in the history of Saudi Arabia is the camel. This animal made travel possible in the barren and frequently waterless desert. The camel of the Arabian Peninsula—the dromedary—has a single hump and flat, thick-soled hooves that do not sink in sand. Because camels have the ability to go without water for several days—and longer if they find juicy plants to eat—they are especially adapted to desert life.

Evidence suggests that horses have lived in the Arabian Peninsula for nearly 3,000 years and have been tamed for the last 1,500 years. A distinctive breed—the small Arabian horse—developed in Saudi Arabia. Over the centuries, the species grew in stamina and speed and

Camels store water, not in their humps, but in their stomachs. Their humps are filled with fat, which can be used as energy when food is scarce. If you'd like to learn more about camels, go to vgsbooks.com for a link to more information about this important desert animal.

later became an ancestor of the Thoroughbred racehorse, prized by horse breeders worldwide. Horses, like camels, have played a very important part in the history of the region. Although horses lack the endurance of camels and have never been used for long desert journeys, they have provided speedy transportation for Arab warriors throughout the ages.

Flamingos, egrets, pelicans, and many other shorebirds are common in Saudi Arabia. The nation's birdlife is mostly migratory—that is, it visits the country during fall and spring as the various species fly between Europe and Africa. The most common bird in the oases is the bulbul, a songbird that appears often in the popular poetry of the country. Eagles, vultures, and owls are also frequently seen, as are crows, black kites, and sparrows.

Natural Resources

Saudi Arabia's most profitable natural resource is its vast petroleum deposits. Hundreds of millions of years ago, the waters of the Persian Gulf covered much of eastern and northern Saudi Arabia, as well as Kuwait and parts of Iran. During the time that this land was under water, vast quantities of dead plants and animals were deposited in layers on the sea floor. Eventually, the land rose, the gulf shrank, and large areas that had been submerged became dry. The pressure of the earth slowly changed the natural deposits into oil. The gulf area contains more than 25 percent of the world's known oil reserves.

As a result of the abundance of oil, the Saudis have developed liquid propane gas and several petrochemicals, such as fertilizers, paints, solvents, plastics, and explosives. Besides oil, the most commonly found minerals in Saudi Arabia are gold, silver, and copper. Bauxite (from which aluminum is made) ranks second to petroleum in volume. Other minerals—including zinc, nickel, pyrite (used in making sulfur), phosphate, uranium, tin, chrome, and lead—have been found. In 1988 the Saudis reopened the ancient gold mines at Mahad al-Dhahal and at al-Masane. Plans are under way to double gold production.

Although oil and its by-products are the lifeblood of Saudi Arabia's economy, the kingdom has explored other sources of energy, especially solar energy. The government has provided funds for research on and the development of solar-powered desalination plants and air-conditioning systems.

◗ Environmental Concerns

The development of natural resources that has led to Saudi Arabia's wealth also poses a threat to the country's environment. The country's high production of oil, including drilling and shipping via pipelines, barges, and tankers, carries the risk of oil spills. To date, the marine environment of the Persian Gulf has suffered more harmful

An **oil rig** stands tall against desert sand dunes. Saudi Arabia's vast petroleum deposits are a major source of the country's wealth, but producing oil also poses a serious environmental threat.

CORAL REEFS

Beautiful coral reefs lie in the waters of both the Persian Gulf and the Red Sea bordering Saudi Arabia. Yet coastal development, pollution, and shipping traffic all harm the health of these marine systems.

Nature itself can also harm coral reefs. In the late 1990s, El Niño and La Niña (disruptions of ocean-atmosphere systems in the tropical Pacific that affect weather around the globe) created dire consequences for coral reefs in the Persian Gulf. The temperature changes in the Gulf waters created coral bleaching—a reaction to stress (caused by either natural or human disturbances) that weakens and sometimes destroys the corals. Approximately 35 percent of the coral reefs in the Persian Gulf were harmed during this bleaching episode. They are unlikely to recover.

effects from such spills than has the Red Sea.

The region has suffered numerous oil spills since the 1980s, including spills resulting from attacks to oil tankers during the Iran-Iraq war (1980–1988). The worst spill, however, occurred in early 1991, during the Persian Gulf War. Iraq purposefully pumped more than five million barrels of crude oil into the Gulf. Although more than one million barrels of oil were recovered, this is the worst recorded oil spill in world history.

The production of oil also creates a by-product of salt-laden wastewater, which is then dumped back into the Gulf and threatens the health of marine life. Saudi Arabia has taken steps in recent years to protect its people, deserts, and sea from pollution while also increasing its production of oil.

◉ Cities

Although many of its people have traditionally been nomads and village dwellers, Saudi Arabia's cities are growing quickly. The success of the nation's petroleum sales has resulted in the development of processing facilities, management and business centers, and workers' housing projects. Not all Saudi cities are new, however, and the country's ancient Arab culture has strongly influenced its long-established cities.

The **city of Riyadh** is home to more than 3 million people. Many Saudis who once lived as nomads have traded their traditional lifestyle for the more settled life of city dwellers. For a link to the most up-to-date population figures for Saudi Arabia, go to vgsbooks.com.

RIYADH The seat of Saudi Arabia's monarchy is located in an oasis in the Nejd region. Oil wealth has enabled planners to guide the city's development. Spacious roadways and modern steel-and-glass buildings dominate the capital, and the population has risen from 8,000 residents at the beginning of the twentieth century to more than 3 million in the early 2000s. In addition to being the business headquarters for the oil industry, Riyadh is also prominent in the manufacture of cement, plastics, and prefabricated houses.

MECCA The religious capital of the country and the most sacred city for Muslims throughout the world, Mecca is the birthplace of the Islamic prophet Muhammad. Situated in a rocky valley of southern Hejaz, Mecca has a population of about 960,000 people. Because of the hot, dry climate of the area, few farms exist near the city, and, except for the manufacture of religious articles, there is little local industry. In ancient times, Mecca was located at the crossroads of caravan routes, making it an important market town. In modern times, Mecca's wealth depends on the visits of religious pilgrims from all over the world. Several million Muslims make the journey each year, and the challenge of housing and feeding them is enormous.

MEDINA Saudi Arabia's second most important sacred city is Medina, to which Muhammad fled in A.D. 622, when the residents of Mecca grew hostile toward him. Medina has more than 600,000 people and is located at an oasis that produces dates, other fruits, and grains. Medina is the site of the Islamic University, which is an important school for Islamic studies. Nearby is the Medina Library, which contains Arabic texts on religion, geography, and medicine. The most valuable book in this institution is an edition of the Quran (Koran—the Islamic book of holy writings).

Saudis crowd the **souk** in Jidda.

JIDDA'S SOUK

Jidda's renowned souk, Souk al-Alawi, is a great sensory experience. The scents of freshly roasted nuts and savory spices fill the air. Shoppers can choose from a vast selection of gold jewelry, incense and spices, and rugs and handmade garments. Traditionally, souks have been a place for Bedouin nomads to sell their handmade goods, as well as a market for food and home furnishings. Souks served as both a trading place and a social center, especially for women. In modern times, however, souks have become a site for buying specialty items or for recreational shopping.

It is handwritten on parchment and dates from the seventh century A.D.—when the religion of Islam began.

JIDDA Situated on the Red Sea in Hejaz, Jidda is Saudi Arabia's administrative capital and one of the country's leading seaports. Its 2 million inhabitants are of many ethnic backgrounds—Arab, Persian, African, and Indian. Rugs and religious articles are manufactured locally, but the biggest source of income comes from religious pilgrims. About 90 percent of all pilgrims traveling from foreign lands to Mecca enter Saudi Arabia through Jidda's port. Jidda also has the country's largest souk (marketplace).

DHAHRAN Headquarters of the Saudi Arabian American Oil Company (Saudi Aramco), Dhahran is an oil hub in the al-Hasa region, where much of the country's oil exploration and processing takes place. With a population of about 73,000 people, the city has developed rapidly since the discovery of oil and features air-conditioned, prefabricated houses and supermarkets that contrast sharply with the surrounding desert.

HISTORY AND GOVERNMENT

The development of Islam in the seventh century A.D. was such a pivotal event in the history of Saudi Arabia that much of what happened before Muhammad's birth is not well studied. Only since the 1960s have archaeological expeditions begun to explore the history of the Arabian Peninsula's early peoples.

Ancient History

The earliest traces of the inhabitants of Saudi Arabia come from the coast of the Persian Gulf, near the city of Dhahran. Archaeologists have found evidence there of a settled, agricultural people dating from about 5000 B.C. The majority of the people in Saudi Arabia, however, are the descendants of nomads who lived near the oases and who roamed the deserts in search of grazing areas for their herds. These residents of the Arabian Peninsula spoke a Semitic language that eventually developed into modern Arabic.

Many nomadic Arabs, probably in search of food, migrated to the

region northwest of Arabia. In about 3500 B.C., groups of Arabs settled in the Sinai Peninsula and in Egypt. Another migration of Arabs went northeastward into Babylonia (modern Iraq). Later, in about 2500 B.C. and again in 1500 B.C., waves of nomadic Arabs settled in the Fertile Crescent (a semicircle of land from the southeastern Mediterranean coast to the Persian Gulf).

The Dilmun civilization flourished along the coast of the Persian Gulf around 2000 B.C. The inhabitants of Dilmun traded with regions that are in present-day Iraq and India.

◉ The Growth of Trade

Many descendants of the Arab migrants returned to the Saudi Arabian region (simply called Arabia) beginning around 1200 B.C. They became merchants and traded spices from India; ivory, animal skins, and slaves from Africa; and jewels, gold, and incense from Arabia itself. Starting from southern and western Arabia, a network of important caravan routes crossed the Arabian Peninsula to Egypt, Syria, Babylonia, and elsewhere in the Middle East.

Early inhabitants of what would become Saudi Arabia transported precious commodities from the south to more densely settled areas in the north and the west. These communities wanted the products that southern Arabia had to offer, as well as the goods that came from eastern Africa and India by overland routes and by sea.

The Sabaean people—traders from southeastern Saudi Arabia—prospered from the tenth century to the first century B.C. In about 350 B.C., the Nabataeans in northwestern Saudi Arabia and present-day Jordan gained control of some of the commercial caravan routes. Because of difficult navigation in the northern half of the Red Sea, many ships stopped along the Arabian coast to unload goods for the caravan portion of the journey. Caravan cities like Jidda, Mecca, and Medina grew as trade centers and provided pack animals, food, and lodging to traveling merchants. Camels, originally raised as dairy animals, became the most common means of land transport.

Eventually, Egyptian, Greek, and Roman merchants cut into the Arab control of the sea routes, and Arab leadership in trade declined. Within Arabia, the kingdoms that controlled the caravan routes became less unified, with individual caravan cities and independent

Caravans of camels and traders crossed the desert of the Arabian Peninsula, bringing goods from as far away as India and Africa to trade at markets.

nomadic groups wielding more power. Arabia continued to be a commercial crossroads but secured fewer profits because of infighting among Arab tribes for control of the trade routes. In the mid-sixth century, the Ethiopians controlled southern Arabia for a brief period, only to be replaced in A.D. 575 by the Persians (from modern Iran).

The Quaraysh people—fighters from the deserts of northern Arabia—gained control of Mecca by the beginning of the sixth century. The religious leader Muhammad was born in Mecca to a family within this influential group in A.D. 570.

The Birth of Islam

Until the age of forty, Muhammad led the life of a well-to-do merchant. In about A.D. 610, however, he began to speak about visions he was receiving from God. According to these revelations, God chose him to teach the religion that came to be known as Islam. Muhammad's visions continued all his life and were eventually recorded in the Quran.

Meanwhile, Mecca continued to attract great numbers of worshipers who kept sacred statues of their gods in a holy place called the

While Islamic artists do not typically render images of **Muhammad,** this illustration from outside the Islamic tradition depicts the prophet who founded the religion of Islam receiving a vision in a cave.

Muhammad's radical ideas about worshiping one god angered the powerful merchant groups in Mecca. He was eventually **forced to flee to Medina,** which became one of Islam's most sacred cities.

Kaaba. The merchant groups of Mecca viewed Muhammad with suspicion. Among other things, he preached the destruction of the statues and called for the worship of the single, invisible God, called Allah. By A.D. 622, Muhammad had made many enemies, who forced him to flee to the city of Yathrib (soon to be called Medina, which means the "city of the Prophet"). Muhammad's escape is called the Hegira, and this event in 622 marks the beginning of the Islamic calendar.

During the rest of his life, Muhammad spread his influence and teachings over much of Arabia, and he and his followers engaged in an activity common to many Arab traders—caravan raiding. Muslim warriors soon gained great wealth and a warlike reputation. In 630 Muhammad returned to Mecca and occupied it easily. He soon destroyed the statues in the Kaaba and turned the site into a holy place for Islamic worship.

With the help of new Muslim converts from Mecca, Muhammad overcame the other peoples of the Hejaz region. Soon, many more were eager to join the powerful and wealthy Muslims. Muhammad became the head of many of these groups, which he ruled from Mecca. By the time Muhammad died in 632, Hejaz, Nejd, and much of the southern and eastern Arabian Peninsula were Islamic.

Want to learn more about Islam? Visit vgsbooks.com for links to websites with additional information about Islam, in-depth articles on events in the Arab world, and detailed material on one of the five Islamic pillars of faith—the pilgrimage to Mecca.

Arab Conquests and Disunity

In the century after Muhammad's death, Arabs began to travel under the banner of Islam to other regions. Islamic Arab warriors conquered Egypt, North Africa, and Spain to the west, and Syria, Mesopotamia (part of modern Iraq), Persia, Afghanistan, and parts of India and central Asia to the north and east.

During these Muslim conquests, Arabia itself began to decline in political importance. The Umayyad clan took over the caliphate (the Islamic religious leadership) in the late seventh century and moved the political center of Islam to Damascus, Syria. (The religious center of Islam remained at Mecca.) Consequently, direct ties between the Arabian Peninsula and conquered lands and cultures were greatly weakened. The Arab peoples in Arabia fell into political disorder, and they fought among themselves.

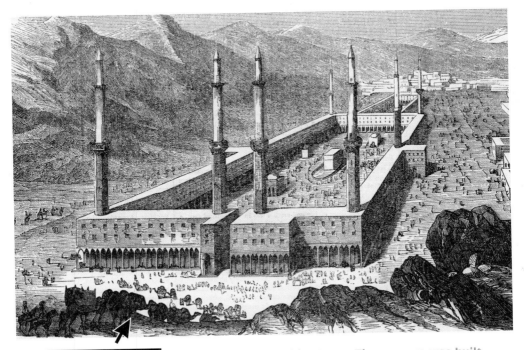

The Grand Mosque, or al-Haram, is located in Mecca. The mosque was built around the Kaaba (meaning "cubic building"), which houses a sacred black stone. Muslim pilgrims come every year to walk around the Kaaba—Islam's holiest shrine—seven times.

In 1453 the Ottoman Turks **captured Constantinople** (modern-day Istanbul, Turkey). At the height of its power, the Ottoman Empire controlled the southeastern Mediterranean, parts of northern Africa, and the Middle East region, including Saudi Arabia.

Through the centuries, many unsuccessful attempts to unite or rule the various Arab groups occurred, but the Arabian Peninsula remained politically fragmented. In the mid-fifteenth century, however, the Saud clan moved into Nejd from al-Hasa, started date plantations, and traded successfully along the caravan routes. The Sauds slowly increased their power throughout the region.

During the fifteenth century, European merchants sought new markets, and for a brief time the Portuguese traded along the Hejaz coast of the Red Sea. Later, in the sixteenth and seventeenth centuries, Ottoman Turks conquered the Hejaz area of Saudi Arabia, as well as Egypt and Syria. The Ottomans maintained distant control of Arabia until the nineteenth century, allowing Arabian clans to rule locally.

The al-Wahhab Family and the Saud Dynasty

During the many centuries of Arab disunity, Islam was generally weak throughout Arabia. The Saud clan in Nejd, however, still followed the teachings of Islam. In the early eighteenth century, a Muslim named Abd al-Wahhab led an Islamic revival movement along with Muhammad ibn Saud, a member of the Saud family. The reform movement—called Wahhabism—was based on a literal interpretation of the

Quran. Its sacred writings strictly limited the use of pictures in religious life and demanded the fulfillment of Islamic laws. The Saud and al-Wahhab families intermarried, strengthening their alliance. During the nineteenth century, these leaders and their descendants conquered most of Arabia, unifying the country and strengthening the practice of Islam.

As a result of Saudi territorial gains, the Sauds came into conflict with the Ottoman Turks. In 1818 Turkish forces, which had seldom ventured into Arabia, invaded and occupied Nejd. The foreign troops were unable to maintain control over the desert fighters, however, and the Sauds reasserted their power in 1824. The Sauds established Riyadh as their capital city.

● Origins of a Nation

The modern history of Saudi Arabia began in 1902, when Abd al-Aziz al-Saud (also known as Ibn Saud) became head of the Saud dynasty, a family that passes on its ruling power to its descendents. He and his followers consolidated Saud control of Arabia. By 1914 Ibn Saud had established full authority over the provinces of Nejd and al-Hasa and was recognized as the leader of Nejd by the British during World War I (1914–1918). By the end of the war, the Ottoman Empire—which had sided with Germany against Great Britain and its allies—completely lost its hold over its Middle Eastern territories.

British forces are pictured *(above)* entering Damascus (in modern Syria) near the end of World War I. During the war, Great Britain and the Ottoman Empire clashed in the Middle East.

After unifying Hejaz and Nejd, **Ibn Saud** *(seated)* became the ruler of the Kingdom of Saudi Arabia, a land traditionally run by various warring groups.

The British were sympathetic to Ibn Saud because he had helped to push the Ottomans out of Arabia. Yet the British gave most of their support to Ibn Saud's rival, the emir (chief) Hussein, ruler of Hejaz. With the aid of the famous British soldier T. E. Lawrence (Lawrence of Arabia), Emir Hussein had revolted against the Ottomans. Hussein then declared himself king of Hejaz. He ruled briefly, however, because Ibn Saud soon defeated him, and by 1925 Ibn Saud extended his own rule over Hejaz.

In 1926 Ibn Saud proclaimed himself king of Hejaz and sultan (ruler) of Nejd, and in 1932 the two areas were united into the Kingdom of Saudi Arabia. Through these actions, Ibn Saud began to dominate Arabian politics and ended the local fighting within the country. He established a firm, centralized rule, and, by strictly enforcing Islamic law, he gradually created a unified country.

Oil Transforms the Desert

In 1933 Ibn Saud granted the right to explore for oil to the U.S.-owned Arabian Standard Oil Company, which later became the Arabian American Oil Company (Aramco). The company discovered Saudi

Arabia's first important well in 1938, and major oil production started in 1946.

Within twenty-five years, the huge income from oil sales brought about many changes in Saudi Arabia. The country that had existed in isolation from the outside world suddenly had international systems of transportation and communication, with airports, television stations, and diesel-fueled trucks.

The rapid transformation took its toll on Arabian culture. Ibn Saud himself lived modestly, but government advisers often mismanaged the money that poured into the country. In 1953 Ibn Saud died at the age of seventy-three, and his eldest son, Saud ibn Abd al-Aziz, succeeded him.

King Saud proved to be a poor administrator and paid little attention to economic matters. By 1958 the government faced difficult financial conditions because of King Saud's policies. The Saudi royal family convinced King Saud to allow his younger but more experienced brother Faisal to run the government.

Faisal, who was born in 1906, had shown administrative ability from the time he was very young. In 1925 he had been appointed viceroy (governor) of Hejaz, and in 1930 he had been given the post of

Faisal *(left)* served as Saudi Arabia's foreign minister for many years before becoming king. In 1947, when this photograph was taken, he traveled to Palestine (modern-day Israel and part of Jordan) on a diplomatic mission.

foreign minister, which enabled him to travel widely, visiting the United States, Spain, and many Arab countries. Between 1958 and 1964, Faisal consolidated his control of the country, and on November 2, 1964, the senior members of the royal family proclaimed him king. The former king, Saud, died in 1969.

The Oil Embargo

Until 1973 King Faisal refrained from serious involvement in the Arab-Israeli confrontation—a conflict that had begun after the Jews established Israel as their national homeland in 1948. In 1973, however, the king assumed a prominent role in world politics after the outbreak of war between the State of Israel and the Arab states of Egypt and Syria.

Faisal was under constant pressure from the leaders of other Arab states to use Saudi oil as a political weapon against Israel. These leaders called for an embargo on, or halt to, Arab oil shipments to nations that supported Israel. Faisal agreed after the 1973 war began, and he reduced oil shipments to European and North American nations. When U.S. president Richard Nixon announced that he planned to increase the flow of arms (weapons) to Israel, Faisal cut off all Saudi oil to the United States and cut back on oil to friends and allies of the

In 1974 **member countries of OPEC** met to discuss crude oil prices. Saudi Arabia was one of the founding members of OPEC.

United States. Other Arab oil-producing nations and some members of OPEC also stopped shipments to the United States.

The embargo caused oil prices to rise from about $8 to $20 per barrel. It created an energy crisis among the industrial nations, some of whom, like Japan and the countries of western Europe, were heavily dependent on Arab oil. After U.S. secretary of state Henry Kissinger negotiated a cease-fire between Israel and its Arab opponents, the embargo ended in March 1974.

Unrest and Regional Tensions

In March 1975, King Faisal was assassinated by one of his nephews. The assassin was later beheaded in public, according to Saudi custom. Faisal's brother Khalid succeeded him to the throne.

Like Faisal, Khalid was a strong leader. He negotiated a border settlement in 1975 between Abu Dhabi (the largest region in the United Arab Emirates), Oman, and Saudi Arabia, and he worked to unify the Persian Gulf states. In addition, Khalid built industrial centers at Yanbu and Jubail, which allowed Saudi Arabia to refine its crude oil at home rather than overseas. Agricultural development, previously ignored by Saudi leaders, was another of Khalid's goals. Wheat production, for example, increased enormously during his reign.

> The takeover of the Grand Mosque was a violent action by conservative Muslims who were committed to retaining Saudi Arabia's strict adherence to Islamic culture and values. The extremists were upset by the kingdom's rush to modernization. They felt such action was compromising Islamic tradition in favor of Western ways.

In 1979 approximately three hundred Islamic extremists captured Mecca's Grand Mosque, an event that rocked the Saud leadership. Rebels held the mosque for ten days before they were removed at the cost of a number of lives. Saudi Arabia later beheaded the sixty-three extremists who had been caught alive. The incident was one of several outbreaks of domestic unrest and rioting that occurred in the late 1970s and early 1980s. In June 1982, King Khalid died, and he was succeeded by his half brother Crown Prince Fahd.

The new king responded to the increasing tensions of the Middle East region by expanding his diplomatic activity and by developing the nation's defense capability. Under King Fahd, Saudi Arabia bought sophisticated military equipment, mostly from the United States and Britain.

In 1981 **the heads of state of six Arab nations**—Saudi Arabia, Kuwait, Bahrain, Qatar, Oman, and the United Arab Emirates—joined to form the Gulf Cooperation Council (GCC).

Another problem the king faced early on was the falling price of oil. As a result of the oil surplus on the world market during the early 1980s, the Saudis earned less money and reduced spending in nearly every government department. The government's debt rose with the decline of oil prices in the mid-1980s.

Saudi Arabia once shared oil rich neutral zones with its neighbors Kuwait and Iraq. The neutral zones grew out of boundary treaties made with these countries in the 1920s. The Saudi-Kuwaiti neutral zone was divided between the countries in 1971, with each country continuing to share equally the oil from the area. Saudi Arabia and Iraq finalized an agreement to partition their neutral zone in 1983.

In addition to its internal concerns, Saudi Arabia continued to seek solutions to the region's tensions. The kingdom joined five other nations of the Arabian Peninsula to form the Gulf Cooperation Council (GCC). In 1987 the council urged warring Iran and Iraq to accept a cease-fire proposed by the United Nations (UN).

In July 1987, another deadly clash occurred during the hajj, or pilgrimage to Mecca, this time involving Iranian pilgrims and Saudi security. As a result of the incident, 402 people died (275 of whom were Iranian) and relations between Saudi Arabia and Iran soured. The relationship between the two countries was already strained due to Saudi Arabia's support of Iraq during the Iran-Iraq war. Iranians held demonstrations and Iranian leaders vowed to overthrow the Saudi ruling family. In early 1988, the Saudi government made two announcements: it would set national quotas limiting the number of pilgrims from abroad during the hajj, and it was severing diplomatic relations with Iran. Iran responded by boycotting the hajj for two years. Following the Persian Gulf War, the countries reestablished their diplomatic ties, and Iranians again attended the hajj in numbers that followed the quota system.

◉ War and Terrorism

In August 1990, Iraq invaded Kuwait, claiming the tiny country as its own. The United Nations Security Council responded by demanding that Iraq withdraw from Kuwait by January 15, 1991, or face military intervention. In the meantime, fearing that Iraq would also try to gain control of Saudi Arabia, the kingdom allowed U.S. troops to enter the country and help protect Saudi oil reserves. When Iraq didn't pull out of Kuwait by the UN deadline, a massive air war was launched by a coalition of thirty-two nations, led by the United States. Saudi bases were used during these attacks. The coalition forces invaded Kuwait and

During the Persian Gulf War, Iraq set fire to hundreds of Kuwaiti oil fields and dumped millions of gallons of oil into the Persian Gulf. These actions caused severe environmental damage in the region.

MISSILES

Although Kuwait and Iraq endured the most damage from the Persian Gulf War, Saudi Arabia did not escape unscathed. Iraq launched numerous Scud missiles at Saudi Arabia (and at Israel) during the six-week war. Approximately 70 percent of the missiles headed for Saudi Arabia were shot down by Patriot missiles, a new technology. The missiles that were not shot down landed in unpopulated areas. No widespread deaths from the Scud missiles were reported.

southern Iraq by land on February 24, 1991, and liberated Kuwait four days later. The Persian Gulf War was officially over.

The end of the war, however, did not mean the Middle East was peaceful. The Saudis found themselves drawn further into regional conflicts in the late 1990s, as several deadly terrorist attacks occurred on Saudi territory. Instead of withdrawing further into isolation, however, Saudi leaders chose to forge new links with regional powers, such as Iran, and to work toward peaceful settlements of disputes.

In late 1995, a car bomb exploded outside the offices of the Saudi Arabian National Guard in Riyadh, where U.S. civilian contractors were training Saudi personnel. The explosion killed seven foreign workers (including five U.S. citizens) and injured sixty others. Several organizations claimed responsibility for the deadly bomb, including the Islamic Movement for Change, which earlier in the year had warned that it would initiate attacks if non-Muslim Western forces did not withdraw from the region. In April 1996, four Saudi nationals were arrested in connection with the attack and were later executed. In 1996 a bomb attached to a petroleum tanker outside the U.S. military housing complex for foreign military personnel near Dhahran killed nineteen Americans and wounded more than four hundred. The Saudi government responded by pledging to increase security

and by offering a reward for information leading to the arrest and prosecution of those responsible for the explosion. No one was ever prosecuted for the bombing, although a Saudi Shia Muslim was suspected to be involved and ties with Iran and Syria were rumored. Saudi Arabia has arrested numerous suspects, but the bombing is still being investigated.

Osama bin Laden, a former Saudi citizen at one time based in Afghanistan, denied involvement in either of these bombings. However, bin Laden and al-Qaeda—an informal international network of terrorist groups of which he is the leader—considered bombing the U.S. embassy in Riyadh in 1994. Bin Laden is thought to be behind a number of deadly terrorist attacks: the 1998 bombings of the U.S. embassies in Kenya and Tanzania; the 2000 bombing in a Yemen port of a U.S. destroyer, the USS *Cole*, which killed seventeen sailors; and the horrific September 11, 2001, attacks in the United States that killed thousands of people, including many foreign nationals. In these attacks, nineteen terrorists (fifteen of whom were Saudis) hijacked four U.S. commercial planes and used them as weapons of destruction. Two of the planes crashed into the twin towers of the World Trade Center in New York City. A third plane crashed into the Pentagon building (the center of the U.S. Department of Defense). The fourth plane crashed into a field in rural Pennsylvania, due to the bravery of passengers who foiled the hijackers and averted a possible fourth attack.

The 1996 bombing at the U.S. military housing complex near Dhahran destroyed the **Khobar Towers** *(left)*.

The September 11 attacks led the United States to spearhead an international coalition to wage war on terrorism, putting pressure on Afghanistan through high-level negotiations with coalition partners to turn over bin Laden and other terrorist leaders. Since the negotiations failed, the United States and Great Britain initiated an extensive air and military land campaign, which began on October 7, 2001. While in support of action against international terrorism, Saudi Arabia, like many Islamic countries, is sensitive to the possibilities of backlash from its citizens, and, therefore, acts with discretion and on limited fronts in fighting terrorism.

Government

Saudi Arabia is a monarchy, and the Quran serves as its constitution. The king, who is both chief of state and prime minister, exercises executive and legislative authority. A twenty-five-member council of ministers is appointed by the king and exercises authority over laws and policy. A ninety-member consultative council also acts as an advisory body.

In the family-ruled house of Saud, power is held by male descendants of Ibn Saud, who founded the kingdom in 1932. The king consults with senior family members over policy matters until they reach consensus (general agreement). *Ulama* (religious scholars) and European- or U.S.-educated business and technical advisers hold minor consultative positions within the government. A crown prince, who will succeed the monarch, is named from among the male descendants of Ibn Saud in order to ensure a peaceful transfer of kingship. The crown prince acts as the deputy prime minister.

Saudi Arabia imposes a death penalty for certain crimes, including murder, rape, armed robbery, and drug trafficking. Executions are sometimes held in public.

The country functions within the framework of Arab tradition and Islamic law. The courts, whose magistrates are appointed by the Islamic leadership, are guided by the Sharia, a collection of religious, political, and social laws based on the Quran and the Sunna (scholarly Muslim writings about Muhammad used in conjunction with the Quran for understanding Islam). The Sharia consists of commentary and explanations of the basic points and rules set down in the Quran. The belief that criminals should suffer at least as much as their victims did determines the severity of punishment. A Basic Law was also established in 1992, which defines the duties and responsibilities of the government. The Basic Law also details rules for passing on authority to second-generation princes.

Political parties and elections do not exist in Saudi Arabia. Despite rapid economic progress, the society remains conservative and religious. Although there is no representative government, a strong tradition of equality among males is present in Arab culture. Consequently, individuals have some rights, particularly the right to make complaints. The king and other royal ministers periodically hold *majlis* (audiences), which allow male Saudi subjects the opportunity to ask for help or to complain about difficult conditions. Female Saudis can make requests only through their husbands or male relatives.

The country is divided into thirteen regions. Village leaders report to regional governors and are responsible to them, assuring a certain amount of central control even in the kingdom's remote areas. Saudi Arabians often choose leaders based on family ties, and one family often dominates a village. Small local groups are headed by sheikhs (chiefs), and when several groups band together, they form a major community whose most important sheikh (decided on the basis of social prestige) becomes the main leader.

SAUDI WOMEN

In Saudi Arabia, men and women are not allowed to attend public events together. They are often segregated in the workplace, and women are not allowed to drive. In 1999 women gained the right to carry their own identification cards. Previously, women were listed on the cards of their nearest male relative. Also in 1999, for the first time, a group of women was allowed to observe a session of the consultative council, although they cannot be appointed to it.

THE PEOPLE

A large proportion of Saudi Arabia's 21.6 million people once were nomads or seminomads, but economic growth has caused the country's settled population to increase steadily. Drawn by the promise of good wages, nomadic and seminomadic Saudi Arabians have moved into cities. In addition, the oil industry has attracted millions of skilled and semiskilled workers—mostly Egyptians, Lebanese, and Palestinian Arabs—from other Arab countries, as well as from Europe and the United States.

In 1998, 7.2 million people made up Saudi Arabia's workforce, 69 percent of whom were foreign workers. A shortage of skilled Saudi workers is cited as a major obstacle in diversifying and strengthening the economy. Part of the kingdom's plan for the future includes educating and training more Saudi nationals for its labor pool.

Nomadic and Village Life

About 10 percent of the population is Bedouin, an Arabic word that means "dwellers in the desert." The largest and most important Bedouin tribes

in Saudi Arabia are the Ataiba, Har, Shammar, Mutair, and Dawasir. These peoples move in search of water and grazing lands for their herds of camels, sheep, or goats. The desert surrounding their pasturelands allows for limited Bedouin contact with other groups and cultures. As a result, their way of life has changed little through the centuries.

Bedouin traditionally live in cloth tents woven from goat or camel hair. Their social organization follows a set pattern—each tent represents a family, a group of families makes up a clan, and a number of clans constitute a tribe. Bedouin are fiercely loyal to members of their group, and they do not readily give loyalty to anyone else.

Bedouin hospitality is another time-honored tradition. According to Bedouin custom, even a stranger must be given food, water, and shelter, because depriving a traveler of these essentials in the desert means certain death. For the first few days, a guest is treated like a member of the family. Custom decrees that after a maximum of three days, the guest's special status expires.

A Bedouin woman and her husband break for coffee on the sands of the desert. Nearly all Bedouins are Muslims.

The separation between nomadic Bedouin and settled farmers or villagers is not absolute. Bedouin depend on settled Arabs for food and tools, which they can obtain only by trading for these items. Also, farmers may become nomadic for the winter months, pasturing their animals in the desert, or they may entrust their animals to nomads to herd.

Villages are established near oases and grow only to the size that the available water supply can sustain. The oases often can support date plantations, fruit orchards, and some cereal (grain) crops. Ethnic groups gather in villages. Some groups have a nomadic branch and a village branch, thus maintaining a nomadic as well as a settled lifestyle.

Urban Life

Saudi Arabia's cities are home to about 83 percent of the population in the early 2000s. Urban planners work to keep traditional Islamic features present in the architecture and organization of urban centers. No longer built of adobe, buildings are made of concrete, steel, and glass in the flowing, geometric designs common to Arab cultures. Residences are built around a central courtyard to give privacy to family members, especially to women and young children. Courtyard walls also offer shade from the sun and protection from high winds. Extended families frequently cluster their homes together in walled-in compounds.

Because of the rapid migration of people to the cities, adequate urban housing is one of the nation's main problems—despite the government's many building programs. The Ministry of Public Works and Housing built thousands of dwellings in the 1980s. Private construction firms also have been active in helping to meet Saudi housing needs. The government is trying to provide living quarters for low- and middle-income groups.

The growing urban areas are a focus for change in Saudi society. Cities were once separated into residential sections according to clan. Groups new to Saudi social organization usually live in the cities. Students, government workers, and technicians are altering the traditional social patterns because these newcomers do not live in locations that are restricted to clans or extended families.

With more people moving to urban areas, **Saudi cities like Jidda *(above)*** are expanding to accommodate a growing number of residents.

Female students at one of Saudi Arabia's universities examine specimens under microscopes. More Saudi women have been attaining higher-education degrees since the mid-twentieth century.

Education and Language

In the past, many Saudi Arabians, particularly the Bedouin and those who lived in small villages, never saw a book other than the Quran. With the increase of wealth from the oil industry, the educational system grew quickly in the 1970s. In the early 2000s, schooling is free in Saudi Arabia and is provided on three levels—elementary, intermediate, and secondary. Commercial, agricultural, and vocational schools offer specialized training programs.

Women account for about 50 percent of the students—a figure that represents an increase of 38 percent since 1960. Boys and girls attend separate schools, even at the university level. Adults without previous education may enroll in a four-year night-school program to study for an elementary educational certificate. The first two years of school are devoted entirely to learning to read and

Education is free and open to all Saudi citizens. Certain restrictions apply to female students, however. Women are not allowed to obtain degrees in engineering, economics, or law. They are often encouraged to enter the fields of teaching or nursing. Once in the workplace, women are rarely allowed to interact with their male colleagues.

write—a policy aimed at improving the nation's literacy rate of 63 percent.

King Saud University, founded in 1950, has a $2-billion campus designed to accommodate 22,000 students. In addition to eight main buildings and a library, the complex has a mosque and a teaching hospital for medical students. The university offers degrees in medicine, engineering science, commerce, agriculture, dentistry, history, mass media, and sociology. King Abdul Aziz University, with campuses in Jidda and Mecca, was founded in 1967. The King Fahd University of Petroleum and Minerals opened in Dhahran in 1963 and is a leading technical institution with students from more than fifty nations.

English is taught throughout the country, but Arabic is the language of instruction. Although Arabic has many local dialects, people from different parts of the country can still understand each other. The written language uses flowing, rounded, and connected characters that are read from right to left.

ARABIC

The official language of Saudi Arabia and of Islam is classical Arabic—a Semitic tongue related to Hebrew and Aramaic. Based on the writings in the Quran, this language relies on the use of prefixes and suffixes. Arabic names, for example, often begin with a prefix, such as *abu*, which means "father of," or *ibn*, which means "son of." To learn more about the Arabic language, see James Robert Smart's *Arabic (Teach Yourself)* (Chicago: NTC Publishing Group, 1992) or Hilary Wise's *Arabic at a Glance: Phrase Book and Dictionary for Travelers* (Hauppauge, NY: Barron's Educational Series, 1987) or go to vgsbooks.com.

A page from the Quran (*left*). Arabic writing is read from right to left.

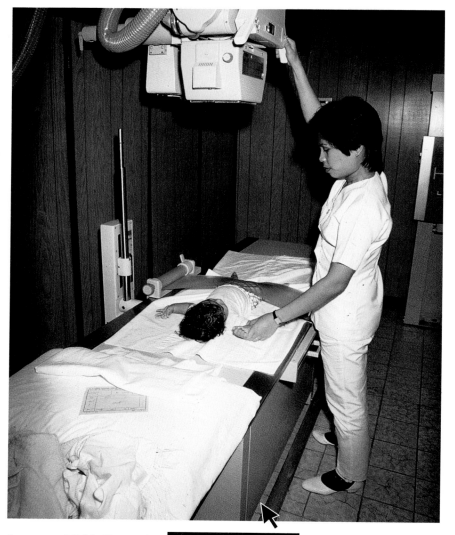

A young child is X-rayed at **Dr. S. Fakeeh Hospital** in Jidda. The hospital is the largest in the Middle East.

Health

Saudi Arabia's chief health problems are typical of those found in many developing countries. But the country has made many improvements in health standards over the years. In 1997, 303 hospitals and more than 1,700 other health centers were in operation. Twenty-three mobile units regularly tour the remote parts of the country. By the early 2000s, the Saudi government was spending more than 9 percent of its budget on health and social welfare programs.

A long-standing health problem has resulted from the yearly migration of religious pilgrims to Mecca. These travelers frequently carry a variety of contagious diseases. As the entry point to Saudi

Arabia for most foreign visitors, Jidda is home to a quarantine center for visitors.

Strict laws have been enacted to curb contagious diseases. Medical workers offer immunization throughout the country, and special mobile teams regularly inspect water and sewer systems. About 95 percent of the population has access to safe drinking water. Various United Nation agencies have helped establish medical facilities that pay special attention to preventive medicine.

The rate of infant mortality in Saudi Arabia is about 46 deaths in the first year per 1,000 live births. The life expectancy—70 years of age—is higher than that of most Middle Eastern countries. Health-care facilities are undergoing huge expansion, and the government provides free, comprehensive medical care. In the late 1990s, Saudi Arabia's medical personnel numbered about 130,000. The government is trying to encourage more Saudis, especially women, to enter the health-care field.

CULTURAL LIFE

Daily life in Saudi Arabia revolves around prayer. Islam also influences, and sometimes dictates, the music, arts, social activities, and diet of the kingdom's inhabitants. Traditions are honored and respected in Saudi cultural life. Yet, change in this highly conservative nation is also apparent in the movement toward a more prominent role for women in society, the introduction of modern technology such as the Internet, and the participation in international sports competitions such as the Olympics and the World Cup.

> For links to up-to-date statistics, current events, and cultural data—including more on the religion of Islam, food, clothing, and places to visit—visit vgsbooks.com. This site also includes links to Saudi newspapers.

Religion

Religion has been the single most important element in the history of Arabia. The birth of Islam in the seventh century A.D. united the inhabitants of the Arabian Peninsula for the first time, giving them a common identity.

Islam rests on five duties: declaring faith, praying five times daily, giving to the poor, fasting, and making a pilgrimage to Mecca at least once in a lifetime. Nearly all Saudi Arabians are Sunni Muslims (a sect of Islam that accepts Islamic leaders who do not descend from Muhammad's family). Most belong to the strict Wahhabi subgroup, which practices a variation of Sunni doctrine. Shiites (those who follow leaders descended from Muhammad's son-in-law) make up about 10 percent of the population. Most Shiites live in the al-Hasa region.

Religious freedom exists in other Muslim countries, but Saudi Arabia only permits Islam. The practice of any other religion is strictly forbidden, except for noncitizens such as foreign oil company employees and

The five daily prayer times of Islam are at dawn, noon, afternoon, sunset, and night. In Saudi Arabia, the exact times for prayer are published in newspapers daily. Schools, stores, and businesses break during prayer time, which lasts for about half an hour.

businesspeople. Non-Islamic religious services, however, are not allowed in public, nor are displays of non-Islamic religious items, such as crucifixes.

The Quran—considered the summary of the revelations by Allah to Muhammad—consists of 114 suras (chapters), which are written in classical Arabic. The book is the main link among the world's 1 billion Muslims.

One of the most important parts of Islam is the hajj to Mecca. Muslims from many countries gather each year to make this sacred journey. During the pilgrimage, all social and political differences among travelers are temporarily ignored. Every pilgrim, whether rich or poor, wears the same kind of simple white garment and participates in the same rituals. Some arrive in Mecca in air-conditioned cars, while others are crowded into huge trucks or buses, and still others come on foot. Women are allowed to attend, but must be accompanied by a man.

Once in Mecca, the pilgrim stops at the Kaaba, a large cube-shaped structure in the center of al-Haram (the Grand Mosque). The Kaaba is

More than 1 million pilgrims come to Saudi Arabia every year for the annual hajj, or pilgrimage to Mecca. Muslims from around the world who are physically and financially able are expected to make the trip to Mecca, site of **the Grand Mosque,** at least once in their lives.

Saudi men practice a **folk dance.**

covered with heavy, dark curtains embroidered with verses from the Quran. Each Muslim circles the structure seven times. Those who are sick or disabled are carried around it on stretchers. Muslims all over the world turn toward the Kaaba five times each day to pray.

The Arts and Communication

According to a strict interpretation of the Quran, music is not allowed in religious services, and often it does not have a place in private life. But

the Bedouin have developed a distinctive chant accompanied by a *rebab* (a single-stringed instrument) and drums. Increasingly, more music is heard in Saudi society, primarily as a result of the influence of radio and television. The newer music is a mixture of traditional and modern styles that are borrowed from other Arab countries. Folk music and dance have become more common in the kingdom in recent years, with more than fifty folk dance and folk music groups.

Representational visual art used to be almost unknown in Saudi Arabia. The Quran is often interpreted to have strict rules against the creation of images—including paintings and photographs—so there is very little painting, photography, or sculpture in the country. Yet, slowly, this is beginning to change. Two female artists, Safiyah Binzagar and Mounirah Mosly, have been fairly successful in introducing their artwork to the Saudi community. The visual

"As we pursue modernization in many aspects of our life and our economy, we don't overlook the value of our religious and cultural roots. [T]hey're the gold in our lives and not to be traded for every trinket in the social and cultural marketplace."

—Abdallah S. Jum'ah, President and CEO of Saudi Aramco

arts have also found an outlet in the making of hand-lettered and illustrated Qurans and in the striking Arab architecture that is based on geometric designs.

In pre-Islamic Arabia, poetry and other forms of literature were widespread. After Muhammad and the coming of Islam in the seventh century, poetic expression declined, because Muhammad did not approve of the romantic verse that was common at the time. The older literature of Arabia is full of stories and poems celebrating romantic love, heroes, war, and the beauty and intelligence of Arabian horses and camels. Poetry and storytelling have been instrumental in preserving Saudi Arabia's history and culture.

Television and radio are popular sources of entertainment. Television shows are varied, consisting of educational broadcasts, readings from the Quran, and entertainment programs produced in Egypt. The voice of a Saudi woman was heard for the first time on the radio in 1963, and since then women have played a more prominent role in the media. Public screenings of movies are forbidden.

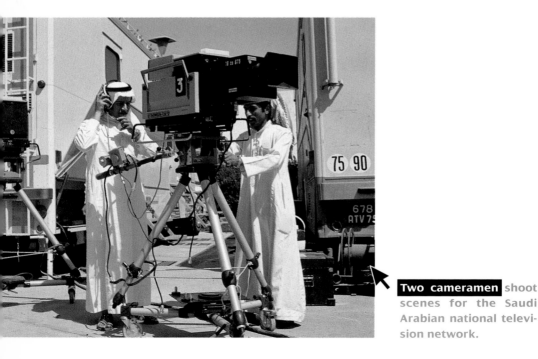

Two cameramen shoot scenes for the Saudi Arabian national television network.

Cell phones are among the various communication technologies to which Saudi citizens have increasing access.

Although Saudi Arabia has had Internet connection since 1994, the Internet has experienced slow growth in the kingdom, due to government regulation that has worked to keep technology from interfering with the traditions and culture of the kingdom. The government has tried to control the flow of information and to block what it sees as inappropriate material that could harm the traditions and culture of its Islamic citizens. Many of the country's governmental offices and prominent businesses, however, host websites, and wealthy Saudi individuals are investing in U.S.-based global telecommunications and Internet technologies.

Thirteen daily newspapers are published in the kingdom, and 185 other newspapers appear periodically. Magazines range from popular publications to literary and scientific reviews. Most of the journals are privately owned but are supported by government advertising and special tax privileges. The government is aware of the activities of the press, and, although there is no direct censorship, newspapers are expected not to publish anything offensive to the state.

◉ Marriage, Social Life, and Customs

Although the Quran permits a man to have four wives—if they are treated equally—most Saudi Arabian men have only one marriage partner. Marriages usually occur between distant relatives and are arranged by the parents. Often the young couple see each other for the first time during the wedding ceremony. Before the marriage is agreed upon, a dowry must be paid to the bride's family by either the groom or his family. Some young people in Saudi Arabia are breaking with these traditions and are choosing their own marriage partners.

A man can easily divorce his wife, by saying on three occasions, "You are divorced from me." He has certain obligations, however, such as providing for the couple's children. It is much more difficult for a woman to obtain a divorce. Although the Quran has many references to the rights and fair treatment of women, they have a less visible and less influential position in traditional Arab society than men do.

> Traditional dress in Saudi Arabia is an example of the country's strict adherence to the Quran. In public Saudi women wear a black abaya (dress) and head covering as a sign of modesty. At home they may appear in colorful clothes and jewelry.

Saudi women wear a **traditional black dress and a veil** that covers the head and face—a requirement in public places.

The **modern Saudi Arabian family** has access to new technologies that weren't available until recent decades. But technology often conflicts with the laws of Islam, which strongly govern the lifestyle of modern Saudis.

Men and women very rarely socialize together—even when close families gather. Saudi women are required to wear veils in public and in the presence of strangers. Generally, women are not welcome in the country's business and political life, but in recent years women have gradually become involved in the medical field and in some social and charitable activities. Public activities in which both sexes participate are almost nonexistent. While men often gather in coffee shops to smoke, gossip, and drink coffee, women do not freely meet outside the home.

Food and Recreation

A customary meal in Saudi Arabia consists of mutton that is served on a large platter with rice, roasted or fried eggplant, salad, eggs, and cheese. Dessert often includes fruit or a custardlike mixture with raisins or almonds. The bread eaten with the meal is soft, flat, and round and is often large and thin enough to be folded over several times.

Because Islam strictly forbids the consumption of alcoholic beverages,

Air-conditioned shopping malls and supermarkets have become common in Saudi Arabia. Credit cards and automated teller machines (ATMs) provide additional convenience for routine shopping trips.

SAUDI FOOD

The culinary palate among Saudis developed according to the foods the dry landscape can support. For example, many dishes are accented with mint and lemon. Olive oil is a staple in the Saudi pantry, as are rice, lentils, and a number of spices. A flat, unleavened bread called pita is served at every meal. Lamb and chicken are common meats. The religious laws of Islam (Sharia) forbid the consumption of pork and alcohol. To learn more about Saudi food, visit vgsbooks.com.

they are unavailable in Saudi Arabia. Even visitors or foreigners working in the country are not allowed to possess liquor. In Saudi Arabia, coffee drinking is a social institution, and whenever Arabs get together, coffee is served. To prepare Arabian coffee, the beans are roasted in small quantities, pounded very finely, mixed with sugar and water, and then simmered in coffeepots. The result is a sweet beverage, scented with cardamom, a gingerlike spice. Tea is also gaining popularity in the kingdom.

Camel and horse racing and hunting with dogs or falcons (hawks) are the favorite traditional sports of Saudi Arabia. Falconery continues among the wealthy.

HUMMUS

Hummus is eaten as a dip, especially with pita bread, or as a sandwich spread. For a dip, hummus is served on a shallow plate and covered with a light coating of olive oil. Tahini, a main ingredient, is available in some grocery stores and at co-ops and specialty food markets.

2 cups canned chickpeas (also called garbanzo beans), drained, liquid reserved

1½ teaspoons salt

4 garlic cloves, minced

⅓ cup tahini (sesame paste)

6 tablespoons freshly squeezed lemon juice (2 lemons)

2 tablespoons water or liquid from the chickpeas

8 dashes Tabasco sauce

Place all the ingredients in the bowl of a food processor fitted with a steel blade and process until the hummus is coarsely pureed. Taste for seasoning and serve chilled or at room temperature.

Standing proudly with his silver medal, **Hadi Souan Somayli *(far right)*** won the 400-meter hurdles event at the 2000 Olympics in Australia. It was Saudi Arabia's first Olympic medal.

Most falcons are brought from Iraq and Iran. These birds are trained to hunt other birds and small animals.

Saudi Arabians also participate in sports popular in North America and Europe. Basketball and soccer have particularly strong followings in the cities and at the oil installations. Exercise programs and gymnastics are part of the physical education courses in school. More than seven hundred athletic clubs offer activities varying from soccer to swimming and from track and field to table tennis. Several modern stadiums have been built. The most impressive sports facility lies in the capital city of Riyadh.

Saudi Arabia also participates in the international arena of sports competition. In 1984 the country made its first appearance at the Olympics, held in Los Angeles, California, with soccer and riflery teams. The national soccer team competed in the 1994 World Cup and won the Asian Cup three times between 1984 and 1996. One of its star players was Majed Abdullah, a striker whose career spanned twenty-two years. The country captured its first Olympic medal in the 2000 Sydney, Australia, Olympics when Hadi Souan Somayli came in second in the 400-meter hurdles.

THE ECONOMY

The greatest single factor of economic importance in Saudi Arabia is the abundance of oil. The country is capable of producing ten million barrels per day but follows quotas set by the Organization of the Petroleum Exporting Countries (OPEC). In early 2000, the quota was eight million barrels per day. As a result of its oil sales, Saudi Arabia has a per capita (per person) income of $6,543, a high figure among large nations in the Middle East. Yet, this figure has fallen steadily since the 1980s, as the kingdom's economic growth has fallen far behind its population growth.

The Oil Industry

The discovery of oil and the development of the petroleum industry by Aramco created the need for new roads, jobs, airports, and housing. When Aramco engineers came to Saudi Arabia, they explored and mapped much of the country for the first time.

Oil revenues increased slowly in the 1950s and 1960s, and the country did not become one of the world's major producers and

exporters until the 1970s. With a rise in oil prices, Saudi Arabia's oil income skyrocketed from $4.3 billion in 1973 to $22.6 billion in 1974. The huge sales enabled the Saudi Arabian government to buy 25 percent of U.S.-owned Aramco, and in 1979, the Saudi government negotiated with Aramco's owners to take full control of the firm, changing its name to Saudi Aramco. By 1981 oil revenues had reached nearly $102 billion.

In the early 1980s, however, a surplus of oil on the world market reduced the nation's revenues. As a result, the country strove to decrease its reliance on oil. Yet, because Saudi Arabia depended on oil for more than 97 percent of its income, the low demand for Saudi oil led to a drop of 18 percent in the nation's gross domestic product (GDP, the total amount of goods and services produced within a country in a year). By 1995 Saudi Arabia's GDP had recovered, climbing to $189 billion.

In the early 2000s, petroleum and petroleum products account for about 75 percent of Saudi Arabia's budget revenue. Other

PRIVATIZATION

The Saudi government is relinquishing control of many of the major economic activities in the country. In 1999, for example, the government announced it would begin privatizing its electricity companies. In 2000 it revealed plans to turn its airline, Saudi Arabian Airlines, into a privately held business. The telecommunications company is also in the process of privatization. This privatization move is designed to stimulate economic growth in the kingdom, particularly in non-petroleum-based industries. However, this plan has met some resistance from the private sector and some members of the royal family, who fear privatization will cause further unemployment for Saudis.

income is generated from agriculture, industry, and services. The country is continuing to make great efforts to become less reliant on oil, including the creation in 1999 of the Supreme Economic Council. This council's role is to boost investment, create jobs for Saudi nationals, and promote the private sector.

Saudi Arabia has proven oil reserves of 262 billion barrels—or about 25 percent of the world's total. The known amount of reserves in Saudi Arabia increases each year as more oil is discovered. By using money from oil sales, the Saudi government has expanded its processing capability and has developed refining and marketing facilities. With the help of several international firms, Saudi Aramco (the country's primary oil producer) is searching for oil in the central part of the country—an area that, so far, has remained largely unexplored.

Although tankers ship Saudi oil to Europe and Japan to be refined, Saudis are refining increasing amounts of their own oil at home. Until 1960 the refinery at Ras Tanura was Saudi Arabia's only processing facility. In early 2000, eight Saudi refineries were in operation.

An oil refinery in Ras Tanura. Saudi Arabia is the world's largest exporter of petroleum.

Combined, these refineries are capable of producing more than 1.6 million barrels per day of refined petroleum products. The kingdom is continuing projects to expand these capabilities.

Pipelines carry some oil to the island nation of Bahrain. Natural gas, a by-product of crude oil deposits, was once considered a useless nuisance. The gas is collected to use as fuel. Natural gas and crude oil (petroleum) account for approximately 60 percent of worldwide energy consumption. In Saudi Arabia, natural gas is piped to purification plants in al-Hasa. In 2000 Saudi Aramco produced about 781,000 barrels per day of natural gas liquids.

Although oil and its by-products are the lifeblood of Saudi Arabia's economy, the kingdom has explored other sources of energy, especially solar energy. It has provided funds for research on and the development of solar-powered desalination plants and air-conditioning systems.

Agriculture and Industry

Agriculture is limited to the Asir region and to oases that have adequate rainfall or sufficient well water. Some areas of Nejd and al-Hasa are being developed, but less than 2 percent of Saudi Arabian land is

From the air, green circles of **irrigated cropland** contrast sharply with the surrounding desert. Only about 1 percent of Saudi Arabia's land is used for agriculture.

used for farming. The prices of Saudi agricultural goods are high compared with average world markets because the water needed to irrigate the land is very expensive to obtain.

The Saudi government is working to extend the country's agricultural potential by funding programs to turn the desert into farmland. This process involves irrigation, proper drainage, and control of surface water and blowing sand. Government funds are used to construct dams, to purify water for drinking, and to establish centers that offer technical assistance to farmers.

Dates, an important food crop, are one of the mainstays of the Saudi diet. This dependency on dates is changing however, as Saudi farmers begin to grow a wider variety of vegetables, fruits, and grains. Especially striking has been the increase in the production of cereal grains. In 1977 wheat production totaled 300,000 tons (305,000 metric tons), but by 1995 this figure had risen to 3 million tons (3 million metric tons)—giving a yearly harvest that exceeded the wheat consumption in the kingdom and leading to the exportation of wheat. Other leading crops are barley, alfalfa, watermelons, and citrus products. Livestock estimates include 7.8 million sheep, 4.4 million goats, 225,000 cattle, 422,000 camels, and 87 million chickens.

A Saudi **farmer harvests onions.** Modern irrigation techniques, introduced in the mid-1900s, have enabled farmers to grow a wider variety of produce.

Saudi Arabia's industrial goods—outside of oil—include cement, plastics, soap, shoes, clothing, and other consumer items. The country still relies heavily on imported goods, food, and machinery. Saudi Arabia's major trading partners are the United States, Great Britain, Japan, Germany, France, South Korea, and Singapore. Industries unrelated to petroleum combine to contribute only 8 percent to the GDP. In 2000 the kingdom was in negotiations to be admitted to the World Trade Organization (WTO). Membership would improve its exportation of both oil and non-oil products.

Transportation

Saudi Arabia's main ports are Jidda, Dammam, Yanbu, and Jizan. Port facilities are expanding to accommodate the increasing flow of exports and imports. Ras Tanura historically was the most important oil-loading port, serving thousands of tankers yearly. On the Persian Gulf coast, large numbers of traditional Arab sailing ships, called

SAUDIIZATION

Unemployment is a concern in Saudi Arabia. The government is trying to respond through a "Saudiization" program, which calls for job growth for Saudi nationals. The goal is to replace 60 percent of the foreign workforce with Saudi personnel. For example, the government has stopped issuing work visas in some industries, has required private businesses to hire a certain number of Saudi nationals, and has increased training opportunities for Saudis. Yet, while the Saudi government takes steps toward the Saudiization of its workforce, Saudi monies continue to flow out of the country into various global investments, such as the Internet, video, fiber optics, and other communications technologies, among others.

A camel hitches a ride in the back of a pickup truck.

dhows, are anchored alongside large oceangoing vessels. Built by hand of the finest hardwoods, the dhows still carry cargoes along the coasts.

Diesel trucks have replaced camels as Saudi Arabia's main means of transportation, although donkeys are still often used in the distant settled areas. About 94,000 miles (151,000 km) of paved roads carry motor traffic. In 1967 the government built a 950-mile (1,500-km) asphalt road connecting Dammam on the Persian Gulf with Riyadh and the Red Sea port of Jidda. A six-lane highway links Mecca and Medina. A 15-mile-long (24-km-long) causeway (a highway over water) linking Saudi Arabia and Bahrain was completed in 1986.

More than four million cars fill the streets and highways of Saudi Arabia. The kingdom imports cars from many countries, including the United States, South Korea, and Japan, and is the fifth largest market for U.S. auto parts. In fact, per capita, Saudis are among the world's highest spenders on automobiles.

Saudi Arabia has a large fleet of commercial aircraft, including eighty-six planes that fly to forty-two foreign countries. The main airports at Jidda, Dhahran, and Riyadh handle large, modern jets. The Saudi

Arabian government built a huge airport near Jidda that opened in 1982. The King Abd al-Aziz International Airport covers an area of 41 square miles (106 sq. km). The site was designed by French engineers who modeled it after Charles de Gaulle Airport in Paris, France. King Khalid International Airport, at Riyadh, opened in 1983, and a third major airport, King Fahd International Airport, opened in the al-Hasa region in 1994. Other smaller airports form an important link in the country's transportation network.

Railways play a minor transportation role in the kingdom, with tracks that extend from Riyadh to Dammam. The railway transported more than 500,000 passengers and 1.6 tons (1.6 metric tons) of freight in 1996.

▶ Water and Energy

One of the greatest problems in Saudi Arabia is its lack of water. Very little land in the country is suitable for farming. The government has built several small dams to conserve water, as well as a large dam at the city of Abha in the south. Underground water reserves provide another source of water.

A huge desalination plant (a facility that removes salt from seawater) operates near Jidda and has a daily processing capacity of 5 million gallons (19 million liters). About 70 percent of the country's drinking water needs are met through its thirty-three desalination plants.

Saudi Arabia's electrical plants have a generating capacity of 21 billion megawatts, mostly for use in the major cities. Many small settlements have their own electrical plants. Many of the generating

Saudi Arabia, a desert country surrounded by salty seawater, depends on **desalination plants** to provide fresh water to the population.

plants are powered by diesel engines, which allow Saudi Arabia to use its vast oil resources to produce electric power. In addition, electrical turbines installed at desalination plants provide energy for domestic use. Plans are also under way for a gas-fired power plant on the Red Sea coast.

◉ The Future

As the twenty-first century begins, Saudi Arabia is experiencing a period of change. New technology such as the Internet and expected admission into the WTO are pushing the kingdom further into the global network and marketplace. In a conservative country built on Islamic tradition and values, such change is likely to cause concern, if not strife.

On the political front, the country is situated in a region of continuing conflict. Isaeli-Palestinian relations are volatile, and violence is epidemic. A charter member of the Arab League, Saudi Arabia supports the Arab position that Israel must withdraw from the territories that it occupied in 1967, including East Jerusalem. The Gulf War of early 1991 forced Saudi Arabia into a confrontation between the United States and Iraq. After the Gulf War, Saudi leaders chose to forge diplomatic links with Iraq as well as Iran while maintaining the country's ties to the United States and European nations. And, with the September 11, 2001, terrorist attacks in New York City and Washington, D.C., Saudi Arabia was again challenged in balancing its relationship with the United States and with the Muslim world.

Economically, Saudi Arabia is enjoying the profits from the rise of oil prices, which began in 1999. Yet, the country knows from experience that the tide may be short-lived and is actively working to improve its future circumstances through an expanded private business sector— including the privatization of many

THE WORLD TRADE ORGANIZATION

The World Trade Organization (WTO), created in 1995, is the successor to the General Agreement on Tariffs and Trade (GATT), which was formed after World War II (1939–1945). With more than 140 member countries, the organization strives to improve international trade through the development of agreements, or rules, of trade. The WTO helps negotiate and administer trade agreements between countries and settles trade disputes.

Neon signs in Arabic highlight the skyline of Riyadh. Saudi Arabia looks to the future while maintaining its ties to the past.

governmental agencies and businesses—and through job growth and training for its citizens. In this way, Saudi leaders are aiming to diversify the economy to protect it from the ups and downs of the oil market. At the same time, the kingdom is working to pay off the debt it accumulated during the period of low oil prices.

Saudi Arabia continues to use its oil profits for the growth of a strong Arab and Islamic nation. The monarchs are careful not to allow modernization and globalization trends to overcome the nation's religious orientation. Amid tensions from both inside and outside the country, Saudi Arabia remains the keeper of Islam's holy places and the spiritual center of the world's 1 billion Muslims.

5000 B.C.	The earliest inhabitants on record settle in the region of Saudi Arabia.
1200 B.C.	Descendants of nomads return to Arabia and become merchants and traders. Southern and western Arabia become part of an important caravan route.
A.D. 570	The Islamic prophet Muhammad is born in Mecca.
610	Muhammad begins receiving visions from God (Allah) about the religion that will become Islam.
622	Because his religious teachings are new, calling for the worship of a single, invisible god rather than the numerous gods exalted at the time, Muhammad is forced to flee to the city of Medina. This escape, called the Hegira, marks the beginning of the Islamic calendar.
A.D. 630	Muhammad and his followers return to Mecca and occupy the city. This marks the beginning of the spread of Islam in the Arab region and beyond.
MID-1400S	The Saud clan moves into Nejd from al-Hasa and slowly gains power in the region.
1500S-1600S	The Ottoman Turks gain control over the Hejaz area of Saudi Arabia, as well as Egypt and Syria.
EARLY 1700S	Abd al-Wahhab and Muhammad ibn Saud lead an Islamic revival movement called Wahhabism.
1800S	The Saud and al-Wahhab families conquer most of Arabia, unifying the country and strengthening the practice of Islam.
1818	Ottoman Turks invade Nejd to reclaim Saudi territorial gains.
1824	The Sauds force the Turks out of the region.
1902	Abd al-Aziz al-Saud (also known as Ibn Saud) becomes head of the Saud clan.
1914	Ibn Saud establishes authority over the Nejd and al-Hasa provinces.
1926	Ibn Saud proclaims himself king of Hejaz and ruler of Nejd.
1932	The regions of Hejaz and Nejd are united as the Kingdom of Saudi Arabia.
1933	The Arabian Standard Oil Company (later the Arabian American Oil Company, or Aramco) begins oil exploration in Saudi Arabia.
1938	The first important oil well is discovered in the kingdom.
1946	Major oil production begins.
1953	Ibn Saud dies. His eldest son, Saud ibn Abd al-Aziz, becomes king.
1960	Saudi Arabia and Venezuela found OPEC (Organization of Petroleum Exporting Countries).

1963 The voice of a Saudi woman is heard on the radio for the first time.

1964 After King Saud leads the kingdom into economic problems, his younger brother Faisal is declared king.

1973 In protest of U.S. support of Israel in its war with the Arab states of Egypt and Syria, Saudi Arabia and other OPEC countries halt oil shipments to the United States and other developed countries, raising oil prices dramatically and creating a global energy crisis.

1975 King Faisal is assassinated by a young nephew. His brother Khalid becomes the new king.

1979 Extremists seize the Grand Mosque of Mecca for ten days. Saudi Arabia gains full control over Aramco and changes the name to Saudi Aramco.

1982 King Khalid dies. His half brother Crown Prince Fahd succeeds him.

1984 Saudi Arabia participates in its first Olympics, in Los Angeles, California.

1990-1991 Saudi Arabia allows a coalition of nations to use Saudi military bases to attack and defeat Iraq in the Persian Gulf War after Iraq's invasion of Kuwait.

1992 The Basic Law of government is adopted by King Fahd.

1993 Saudi Arabia is divided into thirteen regions for administrative purposes. The first consultative council meets. The council is composed of a chairman and sixty members, chosen by the king for four-year terms.

1994 The Saudi national soccer team appears in its first World Cup. The Internet is introduced in Saudi Arabia.

1995 King Fahd has a stroke, and Crown Prince Abdullah al-Saud assumes many of the king's responsibilities. A car bomb explodes in Riyadh, killing seven foreign workers (including five U.S. citizens) and injuring sixty others.

1996 A bomb explodes outside the U.S. military housing complex near Dhahran, killing nineteen Americans and injuring more than four hundred.

1997 The consultative council is expanded from sixty to ninety members.

1999 Women in Saudi Arabia gain the right to carry their own identification cards.

2000 Saudi Arabia and Yemen resolve their border dispute.

2001 Terrorists (mainly Saudis) ram hijacked passenger jets into the World Trade Center in New York and into the Pentagon in Washington, D.C., killing thousands.

COUNTRY NAME Kingdom of Saudi Arabia

AREA 865,000 square miles (2,240,350 sq. km)

MAIN LANDFORMS Hejaz, Asir, Nejd, Rub al-Khali, al-Hasa, al-Nafud

HIGHEST POINT Mount Sawda, 10,279 feet (3,133 m) above sea level

LOWEST POINT Sea level

MAJOR RIVERS No permanent rivers

ANIMALS Cattle, goats, camels, sheep, and chickens are raised domestically. Wild animals include antelopes, gazelles, hyenas, lizards, snakes, baboons, wolves, jackals, foxes, ratels, rabbits, hedgehogs, jerboas, ibex, flamingos, egrets, and pelicans.

CAPITAL CITY Riyadh

OTHER MAJOR CITIES Mecca, Jidda, Dammam, Medina

OFFICIAL LANGUAGE Arabic

MONETARY UNIT Riyal. 100 halalas = 1 riyal

SAUDI ARABIAN CURRENCY

The story of modern Saudi Arabian currency begins in 1932, the year that King Abd al-Aziz al-Saud (Ibn Saud) first began minting coins bearing the name of the newly unified Kingdom of Saudi Arabia. In 1952 the Saudi Arabian Monetary Agency (SAMA) was created to modernize the monetary system in Saudi Arabia. One of SAMA's most important steps in this process came in 1961, when paper money in denominations of 100, 50, 10, 5, and 1 riyals was issued. The bank notes were originally issued to benefit pilgrims making the trip to Mecca, allowing them to carry bills rather than a heavy sack of coins. The notes became popular in all sectors of Saudi Arabian society and are used extensively.

Fast Facts

Currency

The Saudi Arabian flag is inscribed with the Islamic Statement of Faith, "There is no God but Allah, and Muhammad is his Prophet." The inscription was added to the flag in 1901. A sword lies beneath the inscription as a sign of the expansion of Islam through military conquests. The inscription and sword appear on a field of green—the color of Islam, also thought to be Muhammad's favorite color.

The current flag was adopted in 1973, but several versions of the green flag have been used by the Wahhabi sect since the nineteenth century. The flag is considered sacred in the kingdom and must not be flown at half-mast or reproduced on clothing or other commercial items.

Adopted in 1950, the Saudi Arabian national anthem was written by Ibrahim Khafaji. The tune was composed by Abdul Rahman al-Katib. Following is a translation of the anthem:

"Onward toward the Glory and the Height"
Hasten to glory and supremacy!
Glorify the Creator of the heavens
And raise the green, fluttering flag,
Carrying the emblem of Light!

Repeat (the words): Allah is greatest!

O my country,
My country, may you always live,
The glory of all Muslims!
Long live the King,
For the flag and the country!

To listen to Saudi Arabia's national anthem, go to vgsbooks.com or visit:
<http://www.emulateme.com/sounds/saudiara.mid>
<http://www.saudia-online.com/images/saudiantham.mid>

MAJED ABDULLAH (b. 1958) Abdullah was a prized member of the Saudi national football (soccer) team, which won the Asian Cup in 1984, appeared in the Olympics in 1984, and qualified for the World Cup finals in 1994. During his twenty-two-year career, he was also the top scorer in the Saudi Premier League six times. He retired from soccer in 1998.

SAFIYAH BINZAGAR (b. 1940s?) Considered the ambassador of women artists in Saudi Arabia, painter and author Binzagar held her first art exhibit in 1969. Her paintings depict Saudi culture and heritage, particularly that of Saudi women. A museum in her honor, the Darah Safiyah Binzagar, opened in 2000. The museum is also a center of learning for art and culture. Binzagar plans to hold seminars, art lectures, and international exhibits at the museum. She also plans to launch a website.

KING FAHD (Fahd bin Abdel-Aziz al-Saud) (b. 1922) Crowned after the death of King Khalid in 1982, King Fahd was faced with fluctuating oil prices, which continue into the twenty-first century. Under King Fahd's leadership, the kingdom has been continuing the work of diversifying its industries in an attempt to become less dependent on oil. Fahd's reign has also been marked by efforts to privatize many functions in the economy that were formerly under the government's control. King Fahd suffered a stroke in 1995. Since then, Crown Prince Abdullah al-Saud has played an increasing role in meeting many of King Fahd's responsibilities.

KING FAISAL (Faisal ibn Abd al-Aziz ibn Saud) (1905–1975) King of Saudi Arabia from 1964 to 1975, Faisal gained authority over the kingdom during a period of economic trouble. With the goal of modernizing Saudi Arabia, King Faisal strengthened existing universities in the kingdom and opened the College of Petroleum and Minerals (later named King Fahd University of Petroleum and Minerals) in Dhahran. He also worked to stimulate growth while simultaneously calling for a reaffirmation of Islamic principles. The well respected and effective king was assassinated by one of his nephews in 1975.

IBN SAUD (Abd al-Aziz al-Saud) (1880–1953) The first king of modern Saudi Arabia, Ibn Saud gained control over the Nejd and al-Hasa provinces by 1914. In 1926 he proclaimed himself king of Hejaz and ruler of Nejd, and in 1932, he changed the name of the united region to the Kingdom of Saudi Arabia. He allowed Aramco to begin exploring for oil in 1933, a move that led to Saudi Arabia's economic prosperity and increase of power in the political world.

KING KHALID (Khalid ibn Abd al-Aziz al-Saud) (1923–1982) Khalid assumed the throne in 1975 after the assassination of his half brother

King Faisal. King Khalid is remembered as a quiet yet effective leader. He was instrumental in the establishment of the Gulf Cooperation Council (GCC)—an organization of six Arab nations (Bahrain, Kuwait, Oman, Qatar, Saudi Arabia, and the United Arab Emirates) whose goal is to coordinate and unify regional economic, industrial, and defense policies. During Khalid's reign, the country began working toward diversifying its industries, notably through building industrial complexes in Yanbu and Jubail. The nation's military also increased its power under his leadership, with the purchase of sixty F-15s and other arms from the United States. King Khalid was also faced with the 1979 seizure of the Grand Mosque in Mecca. The takeover ended with much bloodshed. Khalid served as king until his death in 1982.

LAWRENCE OF ARABIA (1888–1935) British soldier, adventurer, and writer, T. E. (Thomas Edward) Lawrence was a member of the British Military Intelligence Service during World War I (1914–1918). Stationed in Cairo, Egypt, Lawrence was sent to assist the Arab prince Faisal (later the Iraqi King Faisal I) in capturing Damascus (in modern Syria) from the Ottoman Turks. He became an Arab military adviser and led the Arabs in conquering the Turks. He recorded his experience in the book *The Seven Pillars of Wisdom*. His story can also be viewed in the 1962 film *Lawrence of Arabia*.

MOUNIRAH MOSLY (b. 1952) Mosly is a painter, graphic designer, teacher, and art critic whose work has appeared throughout the Middle East and abroad. The Museum of Modern Art in Madrid, Spain, has displayed her work, as has the National Museum of Women in the Arts in Washington, D.C., and the Barbican Centre in London.

MUHAMMAD (A.D. 570–632) Born in Mecca in A.D. 570, Muhammad is viewed by Muslims as the messenger of God, or Allah. In 610 he began receiving instructions from Allah on how to teach what would become the religion of Islam. During the rest of his life, Muhammad worked to spread these revelations, recorded as the Quran, throughout the Arabian peninsula.

HADI SOUAN SOMAYLI (b. 1976) At twenty-four years old, Somayli became Saudi Arabia's first athlete to win an Olympic medal. He received a silver medal for his second-place finish in the 400-meter hurdles during the 2000 Sidney, Australia, Olympics.

ABD AL-WAHHAB (1703–1792) Associated with the rise of the al-Saud dynasty, Abd al-Wahhab was a Muslim scholar. Outraged by the practice of prayer to shrines and other objects by the Shia sect of Islam, he led the Wahhabi movement, which stressed the Islamic principle of a single God. He eventually worked with the political leader Muhammad ibn Saud to spread this reform movement throughout Saudi Arabia.

Saudi Arabia does not grant tourist visas. The only way to visit the kingdom is to be sponsored by an individual or a business in the country. Muslims making a pilgrimage to Mecca may apply for a religious visa.

JIDDA Jidda hosts one of the best souks (open-air markets) in Saudi Arabia. Souk al-Alawi is a great place to see, smell, and touch ancient Saudi Arabia. Shoppers at souks can buy handmade clothing, rugs, gold jewelry, and spices. Jidda also boasts several museums, including the Museum of Abdel Raouf Hasan Khalil, which house historical and cultural artifacts from the region and around the country.

MECCA Mecca is the site of Muhammad's birth, where he began preaching, and where he returned for his final pilgrimage. Only Muslims are allowed to visit this most sacred city, the destination of the hajj, or pilgrimage, that all Muslims are to make once in their lifetime. (A woman can attend the hajj only if she is escorted by a man.) Once at Mecca, devout Muslims visit the Grand Mosque and pray before the Kaaba. More than 1 million pilgrims visit Mecca each year during the hajj.

MEDINA Saudi Arabia's second holiest city, Medina is where Muhammad fled in A.D. 622, when the residents of Mecca grew hostile toward him. The city is a common stop among Muslims making the pilgrimage to Mecca. Medina is the home of the Prophet's Mosque, which contains the tomb of Muhammad.

RIYADH The capital of Saudi Arabia, Riyadh has become a high-tech city, with a first-class airport and modern glass, steel, and concrete architecture. The city also has fascinating museums, such as the Riyadh Museum (which covers the history and archaeology of the kingdom as well as Islamic architecture) and the King Saud University Museum and Murabba Palace, which displays traditional clothing and crafts. The city's growth and new developments are complemented by preservation work, including the restoration of the ancestral home of the al-Saud clan.

Arabic: the official language of Saudi Arabia and of Islam. Arabic is a Semitic tongue related to Hebrew and Aramaic.

Aramco (Arabian American Oil Company): the American-owned oil company that obtained permission from Ibn Saud to begin exploring for oil in Saudi Arabia in 1933. In 1979 Saudi Arabia bought out the American interest in the company and changed the name to Saudi Aramco. The company is the country's primary oil producer.

desalination: the process of removing salt from seawater

dowry: the money, goods, or property that a groom or his family pays to a bride's family

dynasty: a family that passes its ruling power from one member to another

hajj: the pilgrimage to Mecca that all devout Muslims are to try to make once in their lifetime

Islam: the religion of 90 percent of Saudi Arabia, based on the Quran, as revealed by the prophet Muhammad. Islam is the only legal religion of the nation. Citizens are not allowed to practice other religions.

monarchy: the form of government in Saudi Arabia, where the male descendants of the Saud family head the government

neutral zone: a zone between two countries that neither owns but in whose resources both can share equally. Saudi Arabia once shared neutral zones with Kuwait and Iraq.

OPEC (Organization of Petroleum Exporting Countries): formed in 1960, OPEC consists of eleven countries that produce more than 40 percent of the world's oil. This organization works toward setting production quotas and otherwise controlling the prices of oil for the benefit of its member countries.

Quran: the writings of Islam, as revealed by Muhammad beginning in A.D. 610. These writings were revealed to Muhammad by Allah and consist of 114 suras (chapters). The Quran serves as the constitution of Saudi Arabia's government.

Saudiization: a government plan to increase employment rates for Saudi nationals and to decrease the number of foreign workers in the kingdom. The program includes hiring requirements for private businesses and training for Saudi nationals.

Sharia: the laws of Islam that direct Saudi Arabia's government. The Sharia consists of commentary and explanations set down in the Quran and the Sunna.

viceroy: the governor of a province or region who serves as a representative of the king

Arab Gateway
Website: <http://www.al-bab.com/arab/countries/saudi.htm>
With links to Saudi and U.S. newspapers on recent events, the Arab Gateway provides a wealth of information about the kingdom. Includes maps, biographies, and cultural information.

BBC (British Broadcasting Corporation) News Online
Website: <http://news.bbc.co.uk/low/english/world/middle_east/>
This is a good site to learn more about ongoing events in the Middle East.

Central Intelligence Agency (CIA), *The World Factbook*
Website: <http://www.odci.gov/cia/publications/factbook/index.html>
The World Factbook contains basic information on Saudi Arabia's geography, people, economy, government, communications, transportation, military, and transnational issues.

CNN.com
Website: <http://www.cnn.com>
This is an excellent site for up-to-date articles about current events in Saudi Arabia.

The Europa World Year Book 2000.
London: Europa Publications Limited, 2000.
This annual publication includes statistics on everything from agriculture and tourism to education and population density. It also contains a long, detailed account of Saudi Arabia's history and current events; government; military; economy; social welfare; education; and a list of public holidays. Another survey explains details of the government structure, function, and constitution.

Library of Congress, Federal Research Division
Saudi Arabia—A Country Study
Website: <http://lcweb2.loc.gov/frd/cs/satoc.html>
The Library of Congress presents an analysis of Saudi Arabia's political, economic, and social structure, with an emphasis on the inhabitants of the kingdom.

Lonely Planet World Guide
Website: <http://www.lonelyplanet.com/destinations/middle_east/saudi_arabia/facts.htm>
This guide contains information for visitors to Saudi Arabia, including a list of attractions and events, currency facts and traveling costs, and a brief lesson in Saudi culture.

Population Reference Bureau
Website: <http://www.prb.org/>
The annual statistics on this site provide a wealth of data on Saudi Arabia's population, birth and death rates, fertility rate, infant mortality rate, and other useful demographic information.

***Statistical Abstract of the World.* Detroit: Gale Research, 1997.**
This is the source to turn to for economic and social data worldwide. You'll also find a comprehensive directory of each country's government, diplomatic representation, press, and trade organizations among others.

Turner, Barry, ed. *The Statesman's Yearbook: The Politics, Cultures, and Economics of the World, 2001.* New York: Macmillan Press, 2000.
This source clearly and succinctly presents statistical information as well as the latest details about the country's educational system, administration, defense, and energy and natural resources.

United Nations Statistics Division
Website: < http://www.un.org/Depts/unsd/>
This UN site provides a wide range of statistics, including economic, environmental, social, and demographic data.

U.S.-Saudi Arabian Business Council
Website: <http://www.us-saudi-business.org/>
The purpose of this site is to educate U.S. businesses about life in Saudi Arabia, thereby promoting trade and investments between the two countries.

Washingtonpost.com
Website: <http://www.washingtonpost.com/>
With its archives extending back to 1977, the *Washington Post* online is an excellent source for in-depth articles on the kingdom's recent history. A small fee is charged for downloading full stories in the archives.

ABC News.com—Country profiles
Website: <http://www.abcnews.go.com/reference/
countryprofiles/countryprofiles_index.html>
This site provides background information on nearly every country in the
world. It includes information on each country's history, culture, geography,
natural resources, government, politics, economics, and demographics. Also
included are a map and flag of each country.

Bagader, Abubakr, Ava M. Heinrichsdorff, and Deborah S. Akers, eds.
Voices of Changes: Short Stories by Saudi Arabian Women Writers.
Boulder, CO: Lynne Rienner Publishers, 1997.
A compilation of twenty-six stories by women writers from Saudi Arabia, this
book offers an inside glimpse of the Saudi kingdom. Story titles include "Had
I Been Male," "The Duties of a Working Wife," and "Just Give Me the Right
to Dream."

Briley, John. *The First Stone.* New York: William Morrow and Co., 1997.
This is the fictional story of a young Jewish American woman who is recruited
by the Israeli secret service to become a spy in Saudi Arabia. To do so, she
must marry a rich Saudi and live in his harem (the home of a husband's group
of wives). There she falls in love with her husband and must eventually choose
between him and her people.

**Brown, Anthony Cave. *Oil, God, and Gold: The Story of Aramco and
the Saudi Kings.* New York: Houghton Mifflin, 1999.**
Using documents not previously available to journalists, the author of this book
presents detailed information about the important role of Aramco in the oil
industry and the complex problems the company faced.

Fazio, Wendy. *Saudi Arabia.* Chicago: Children's Press, 1999.
Along with colorful pictures, this children's book (appropriate for readers ages
nine through twelve) presents a well-rounded view of Saudi Arabia. Topics
include the kingdom's history, geography, economics, religion, and cultural
life.

**Foster, Leila Merrell. *Saudi Arabia* (Enchantment of the World).
Chicago: Children's Press, 1996.**
This children's book is appropriate for readers ages nine through twelve and
discusses the history, culture, geography, industry, and economy of the kingdom of Saudi Arabia.

**Lawrence, T. E. *Seven Pillars of Wisdom: A Triumph.* 1935. Reprint,
New York: Anchor Books, 1991.**
This is an account of Lawrence's adventures among the Arabs.

**Lings, Martin. *Muhammad: His Life Based on the Earliest Sources.*
Rochester, VT: Inner Traditions, 1987.**
Using sources from the eighth and ninth centuries A.D., Lings presents a
chronological biography of the prophet Muhammad. This book details the life
and times of the Prophet, including personal and spiritual aspects of his life.

Further Reading and Websites

Peters, F. E. *The Hajj*. Princeton, NJ: Princeton University Press, 1994.
This book is a history of the pilgrimage to Mecca, called the hajj, one of the central religious duties of Muslims. The author has collected firsthand accounts from travelers to the holy city and has shaped their experiences into this narrative.

Royal Embassy of Saudi Arabia
601 New Hampshire Avenue Northwest
Washington, D.C. 20037
Website: <http://www.saudiembassy.net/>
Learn about the history, economy, culture, and government of Saudi Arabia straight from the kingdom's embassy. This website also features information about Saudi Arabia's relations with the United States, as well as numerous photos.

Sasson, Jean P. *Princess: A True Story of Life Behind the Veil of Saudi Arabia*. New York: Avon, 1997.
This is the memoir of one woman's struggles in Saudi culture. A member of the royal family, this woman recounts a life of oppression at the hands of the royal males and religious leaders.

Vassiliev, Alexei. *The History of Saudi Arabia*. New York: New York University Press, 2000.
This analysis of the Saudi state includes detailed descriptions of the kingdom's development over the past two hundred years.

vgsbooks.com
Website: <http://www.vgsbooks.com>
Visit vgsbooks.com, the homepage of the Visual Geography Series®. You can get linked to all sorts of useful on-line information, including geographical, historical, demographic, cultural, and economic websites. The vgsbooks.com site is a great resource for late-breaking news and statistics.

Wilkinson, David Marion. *The Empty Quarter*. Edited by Sarah Nawrocki. Albany, CA: Boaz Publishing, 1997.
Filled with details about the oil industry, this suspenseful novel follows an American worker into the oil fields of the Empty Quarter of Saudi Arabia.

Captions for photos appearing on cover and chapter openers:

Cover: This adobe building is located in the southwestern city of Najran. The region has been inhabited for more than four thousand years.

pp. 4–5 A camel train crosses the desert in a sandstorm.

pp. 8–9 Mountains in the Asir region of southwestern Saudi Arabia rise to about 10,000 feet (3,050 m) above sea level.

pp. 38–39 A group of Saudi men wearing traditional dress congregates in Riyadh.

pp. 46–47 The Museum of Abdel Raouf Hasan Khalil in Jidda houses many historical and cultural artifacts of Saudi Arabia.

pp. 56–57 This photo shows a collection of Saudi Arabian riyals.

Photo Acknowledgments
The images in this book are used with the permission of: © R. Warburton/Middle East Pictures, pp. 4–5, 8–9, 17; PresentationMaps.com, pp. 6, 18; © K. M. Westermann/CORBIS, p. 7; © TRIP/H. Rogers, pp. 10, 11; © TRIP/TRIP, pp. 13, 41, 42, 44, 49, 50, 60, 61; © Wolfgang Kaehler/CORBIS, pp. 14, 46–47, 51, 56–57, 64–65; Exxon Co. USA/American Petroleum Institute, p. 15; © E. Bjurstrom/Middle East Pictures, pp. 16, 38–39, 40, 62; © M. Dutton/Middle East Pictures, p. 19; © North Wind Picture Archives, pp. 22, 24, 26; © Bettmann/CORBIS, pp. 23, 28, 29, 30, 58–59; © CORBIS, p. 25; The Trustees of the Imperial War Museum, London, p. 27; Kuwait Ministry of Information, Safat, p. 32; Department of Defense, p. 33; © Reuters NewMedia, Inc./CORBIS, pp. 34–35; Courtesy of the Turkish Republic, Ministry of Culture and Tourism, p. 43; © AFP/CORBIS, pp. 48–49, 55; © David & Peter Turnley/CORBIS, p. 52; © Bill Gentile/CORBIS, p. 53; Royal Embassy of Saudi Arabia, Information Office, p. 63; © Todd Strand/ Independent Picture Service, p. 68; Laura Westlund, p. 69.

Cover photo: © Jeremy Horner/CORBIS. Back cover photo: NASA.